AMERICAN TATTS

AMERICAN TATTS

Linh Dinh

chax press 2005

ISBN 0925904-54-6
CORRECTED, REVISED, AND ENLARGED EDITION

Printed in the United States of America

Published by
Chax Press
101 W. Sixth Street
Tucson, Arizona 85701-1000

Poems from *American Tatts* have appeared in *American Letters and Commentary, Booglit, Editor's Picks, Joss, Octopus, New American Writing, Philadelphia Independent, Schuylkill Valley Journal, Skanky Possum, West Wind Review,* and *xconnect.*

Supported by Tucson Pima Arts Council and by the Arizona Commission on the Arts with funding from the State of Arizona and the National Endowment for the Arts.

Contents

A Blue Pain

"A blue pain will come to us all," the infant lisped.
Soul rhymes with toes, Goethe with sleet.
I have gorgeous blue eyes. "Check this out!" he said,
As he gouged my right eyeball from its socket.
With my left eyeball, interested, I watched him poke
An unfiltered Camel through my blue pain,
Then smoke the cigarette.

Cadavalier

You know what I like about these shoes? The color!
You know what I like about these eyes? The texture!
The color! The texture! I'm by far the richest
Man/woman in the world, by a mile:
Luxurious, bouffant, obscene. (No sex.)
This pinkish universe is really nothing
But a flocculation of my desires.
And yet, nobody!
But nobody but PLEASE!
PLEASE! PLEASE! PLEASE! PLEASE!
Do no more for me, I beg you, come here.

The Undead

Are you presented live before a teeming audience?
Do you stand forth?
Are you adaptable to leisure in a suburban home?
Is motion still imparted to your lips?

I am no longer alive to the risks involved.
I am dead white.
I am a compost of mineral matter.
I am naturally without life, inanimate.
My arms dangle at my sides.
I am neither vital, nor warm, nor interesting, nor bright, nor brilliant.
I am a sweaty handshake at a quiet party.
I am without power or movement. I am exact.

Pick-Up Lines

1
I will stand on tip-toe,
Tape peacock feathers to my forehead.
I will pant half notes,
Speechify in dialect.
I will lather you with my swerved voice,
Peer into your pharynx, weep.
I will wiggle my index finger.

2
Deep down, I know, believe me, about your innermost
Character, feelings, or inclinations, the essential
Or most vital part of your younger self, your thing,
Your older self, the leafy rosette at the heart of
Your cabbage. By rote or by memory, I have,
Trust me, the deepest concern for that burning
Discomfort behind the basement of your sternum,
The spasm at the lower end of your esophagus.

3
Come, let us lie down on the timothy.
Your mud is my manna, we are intimate.
You listen to my effluvium.
There shall be no sanctimony between us.

Doing The Wave

Love, marginal love, I was making love
On the side, as it were,
On the berm at the bottom,
Between tugs. A tumbril
Had brought us here at eight this morning,
Me and my widow.
My dulcet feather,
If we jump up and down together,
Like this, look!
We can make the floor shake.

Rice On The Head

Move into my shed? So there,
In our abscess of helplessness,
I carry you. You
Carry me. We both carry
Our little Arfernee,
Who will soon be big enough,
Tall enough, to despise us
Thoroughly
For our formulaic convictions,
Sans paroles: a father's labor
Is like a schist;
A mother's labor
Is like a schist.

What's At Frank's?

A fake Calder floats over Sheila's head,
Who really should be called Sheila-na-gig,
Because she's all vulva and all suds,
And because she's well-tipped each evening.
On one side of the horseshoe bar is Gummy Christ,
Well-known for his toothy grin, sucking
On a yellow Corona between throws at cricket.
On the other side of the horseshoe bar is Skinny Dave,
Who's all coked-out and skull-plugged
To a quiet walkman playing Nine Inch Nails.
A large trust fund has allowed Dave to be fulfilled
By volume after volume of the fattest sci-fi
He reads zealously while swiveled on his stool.
Dave prefers the ladies' to the men's room,
Because you can be locked inside, although
The full-bladdered matrons are none-too-happy
Queuing outside waiting for Skinny Dave
To finish powdering his fuckin nose.
"Full pelvic undulation will help to dissolve
All neurotic personal armor," someone has written
With a Magic Marker over the broken sink.

Which Not

The man on my left stank so much I had to
Chain-smoke Lucky Strikes to cancel his funk.
"We're all the same," he'd been muttering,
In a castrato voice, odd for a nose tackle,
"You've got to thank God for everything."
The grimacing woman across the bar
Suddenly waved in my direction, grinned,
Became a little less shopworn. I wobbled
Before waving back, smiled,
Before I heard a baritone bellowing
Behind my back: "Sorry I'm late."
The guy on my right cleared his throat:
"I've just moved to Center City
A month ago. I'm still trying
To figure out which bars are cheap. Which not.
Which bars are queer. Which not.
When I came in here and saw no women,
I thought maybe Frank's a queer bar,
But all youse guys are just too pitiful-looking.
Queers like to dress up, from my experience.
Not you, pal."

Watching The Winter Olympics At McGlinchey's

Jackie, who used to be a DJ on WKDU,
The best punk station in Philly,
Is sitting at a booth reading Sophocles.
The translation is bad. She's holding her head.
Wendy, the bartender, has two rows of broken teeth
And an oil derrick inked onto her freckled arms.
She's into Tolstoy, Imperial Russia and the occult,
Whatever's not of this world, at least not of 9 PM,
Although that clock is usually fast.
When Al showed up, Tommy yelled, "Hello, penis head!"
"Yo, cum breath!" "What's up, Al!" "How you doing, Al?"
Al's a balding nurse who method-acts during his spare time.
Our TV has recently been upgraded and now has closed-captions
For the mentally ill. It is, again, the Winter Olympics,
And rebels in Nagano are dying their black hair auburn,
And there's a German guy by the name of Hackl,
With a thin moustache, who has just won something.

Line Breaks

A woman walks into a doctor's office with a carrot
Up her nose, a cucumber in her left ear
And a banana in her right ear.
A guy was riding in a limousine when he saw a man eating grass
By the side of the road.
The day before her abortion,
The one-eyed lady accidentally swallowed her glass eye.
"I notice that your eyes are bloodshot. Have you been drinking, Sir?"
"And I notice that your eyes are glazed, Officer.
Have you been eating doughnuts?"
"Put your coat on. I'm going to the pub for a drink."
"Are you taking me with you?"
"No, I'm selling the house."

The Endless Bar

All claims of the endless bar (except one) are bogus. There is only one endless bar, and that's at 15th and Spruce in Philadelphia. The one in Sausalito, California is not endless. I've seen both ends of it more than once. Ten years of my life I wasted in that dump.

From the outside, The Endless Bar looks ordinary enough: the brown neo-Greek pediment over the narrow doorway; the stained glass windows; the chalkboard advertising 99-cents draft beers during happy hours. Look carefully, though, and you will see the pink smudges of the drinkers' faces pasted against the stained glass windows.

Repetitive, thumping music, the lullaby of the masses, echoes from inside the glass door. You can hear them howling already. Are you sure about this? What the hell, I still have my whole life ahead of me.

Ignoring the faux vet with an orange face, you walk in. It will take decades to befriend these losers.

Are you from around here?

Where are them dancers I've heard so much about?

No ball games tonight.

The endless bar extends—no, *yearns*—into the hazy dark. The faces are like smoke in here. You can only make out the nearest: Samantha.

What did you say your name was?

Samantha is drinking non-alcoholic. A sweating bottle. I just like the heft of it in between my bony fingers, she whispers.

Emphysema, not sex, or maybe both.

Green eyes like marbles in a fish bowl.

Once beautiful.

Her profile is aging audibly, like crackling bark in a bonfire. I'll save you for later, you smiled. I'll be at the end if you need me.

Nice to meet you.

Yo, slimfast! Send me a Morse code, buddy!

I know it was another continent, half a century ago, and I didn't mean to do it, but I'm sorry I punched you, man!

What more do you need? A warm mug, a bag of peanuts, a game on TV, your face in the mirror...

A thousand kinds of beer, all smelling like cold sweat in the morning, next to a strange, groggy face, all good enough to fill up your swirling eyeballs for the night.

And so many mouths in here, all scheming for a raw confession. Do I see a dry hand under a wet table? Excuse me while I go drain this monstrosity!

And what does this place smell like? A soggy photo of a B actress? The corner of Market and Beale in San Francisco at 5:35 AM on April 10th, 1998? The last car on the 7 train at midnight as you stare out the window at Roosevelt Heights?

Your eyes, my eyes. I go there, you go there. Who are these strangers who are squatting in no one's living room?

This boy perches on this wobbly stool all day to peruse sci-fi's, man, anointed by a trust fund. He tried art and literature before he discovered Zen, before he discovered Sufism.

He sampled archeology, anthropology, axiology and cybernetics.

He was a part time student at the Jung Institute.

When he wasn't too drunk he also sculled in the evening.

But he gave everything up to devote himself to the fifth dimension. Between lookouts for a preternaturally bright, rotating disc, he mellows out by analyzing statue-of-liberty draw plays. He has memorized the batting average of every sure-fire prospect who has ever slapped a high and wide through a drawn infield.

You're not being fair (burp), this is what this country here is (burp).

There's an endless bar on every street corner in every endless city. Where else can you chatter up after punching out?

How you girls doing?

Fuck off, faggot. We're not hunting mushrooms tonight. Last night, yes, and maybe tomorrow night.

Until her twelfth beer, she's a lesbian, alright.

You want some?

I'll give you a rain check.

I was adopted, I think.

Are you my mother?

Innumerable clocks on the endless wall. None with arms or numbers, however. They resemble pale moons over a yellow lake. It's not last call until last call.

The bathrooms are leased by the minutes here.

Your nose has been drawn on the wall.

The lights are about to flicker.

Do you want to come home with me?

M/F

I spot her at a nightclub. I have muscles. We will be alone. Perhaps I will offer her a ride home or an invitation to my place. Or I may walk into her apartment as a plumber or a policeman.

I feel shortchanged. As a drinker, I am passionate and artistic. I always look for the right opportunities. I am spontaneous and passionate.

I have no muscles. She lives near me. I look. In the wee hours, there will be an open window. Because I am her lover, I will ask her to put on something sweet.

I can be charming and intelligent. We will be together for several days. It's a step-by-step procedure I've rehearsed. I've only done this a few times. Check out these photographs.

Suggestions

Your nude models are gorgeous
And outstanding. Somehow
We all want to see these pretty angels
Put into embarrassing situations.

Being absolutely nude (no clothes & shoes)
In public while everybody else has clothes and shoes
Is truly embarrassing.

We would like to see them in tough situations too,
Like walking barefoot on snow, dirty alleys or rocky terrain.
Please

Show some pictures of their soles afterwards.
Showing soiled soles in public is embarrassing
And interesting.

My suggestion would be a naked girl
Or even two naked girls wandering
Around naked in a zoo.

The climax would come when the girls
Enter the animal-petting section, where visitors
Can feed and play with animals like goats, etc.

I think the only thing more beautiful than a nude woman
Is a pregnant nude woman. Can you do a photoshoot
Of a nude pregnant woman in public?

There have been a few suggestions
About having the girls nude near children,
As children would have a more obvious response
To a nude girl, how about it?

A girl working with a spade in muddy earth.

A day on the farm, working with the animals,
Tractor-driving and riding a quad bike
Would make an interesting nude day
For a girl.

Nice as it is to see nude girls in public,
There's a lot more fun to be had in watching girls
Lose their clothes either by being forced
To take them off or by losing them somehow.

It'd be nice to get a shot of their embarrassed looks
As they realize they are showing everything they have.

I would like to see that.

First Love

Me and this going down on each other
All summer and once we were
In the bathroom and her sisters
Looked under the door and they were like
You have him head huh?

*

I was on a 6-week course and I met
This girl three days into the course.
I chatted her up during the day and soon
I was in her room to have a cup of coffee.
She was a bit shy at first but that shyness
Disappeared and soon we were all over each other.
We kissed and cuddled for some time
Before we went over to doing it.
She was a bit hesitant but then she relaxed
And I had my first swim in the ocean that night.
It was the most enjoyable experience ever and
Her body became a regular stop for me
While the course was still running.

*

I was 18 she was 15 we were naked in her mom's bed
She said lick me it was very smelly then she said
Shall I do it to you? She sucked me for 6 years every day
She said let's get married I dumped her big regrets now.

*

Ay hello wsup im 14 years old
and well anyways my first time
was very unusual because my g/f
was juss laying their rollin her eyes
like she didnt feel anything but at least
i fuuuuuuuccccckkkkeddddd her up the as
uuuhhh it felt soo good daym fuck yea
uhh yea give it to me bitch yea uh uh uh.

You Don't Know What's Inside Of Me Yet

We were so close to saying it but he promised me the next time
would be the last time so it's understandable
why he's scared of saying THAT.
I'm not saying the L-word first. Hell no!!!
But if we feel that way so soon
and we know that it's not fake. Is it bad?
Later he explained that he was so happy
but that he felt a strong urge to cry because he was leaving me
to move across the country.

*

Church is never as bad as I thought it would be
although it went on half an hour longer then usual.
This old lady came from Cleveland to lecture us about homeless kids.
Very boring.

After church we went to some garage sales
and Dad bought me a turkey sub from Tubby's.
The guy behind the counter wanted to get into my pants.
I could see how his grinning eyes were skimming over my body.
I felt so uncomfortable so I stood behind my Dad.
I felt voilated. So nakid.

*

As soon as everyone left he started groping me
and he wanted me so bad we were in my backyard
and then he pinned me up against the fence and took off my bra
and felt my boobs and I snuck him inside and he banged me
then I gave him head twice and it felt so good
when he got on top of me and we started having dry sex
he kept humping me and I could feel his penis just wanting to come
but he doesnt wanna a gf right now but hes fun to fuck round with anyway
god he made me so wet and I wanted him so baaaad!!!

Two Captains

The captain of the football team, all alone for little old me,
Captain of the varsity cheerleading team! Score!
I showed up, knocking on the door as his mom answered
Saying that she had to go to work, and walked out the door,
As she gave me a knowing wink. God, she's great!
After she left, Sam turned on Spongebob Squarepants
And I made myself comfortable in his mom's pj's. Hee hee.
I'm such a BAD girl! I'd been having wet dreams about his fucking sweet,
Perfect, tan, cut, virgin body ever since I first saw him.
I laid down next to him and stared into his eyes, commenting
On the baby blue they contained. God, he's perfect, and I mean perfect.
All of a sudden, he kisses my cheek, I took the hint, kissing him back
Hard and strong. He sat up to take off his shirt, exposing his gorgeous pecs.
God, fuck me! His mom's pj's were a little too big so they came off halfway.
God, fuck me! In the midst of rolling around on the bed, he gently took my hand
And placed it on the monster bulge in his NAVY sweat.
My gasp erupted into a moan of pleasure no guy had ever given me, ever.
Before I knew it, we were dry fucking so rough I thought I was going to hurt
The poor guy, but no, he only answered back with a huge moan that made
My senses roar. I love to hear guys moan. Love it. His sweet, deep voice
Whispered my name over and over into my crazy head, tugging those pj
Bottoms just far enough for his rough, football-playing hand to pertrude into
My tight pussy. Endorphins crowded my senses, my cum along with his.

29

Dewey in Bucks County

The last great book I read was The Stand, probably, but I read the
Bockman Books at the same time and I honestly can't tell ya which
Book is better, they are both great books.

I'm not mature enough to look at the "bigger" picture.
Why would I want to learn from my mistakes?
I've never lied and I've never been "humbled."

I like any scene with Brad Pitt in it.
I am often told I look like Reese Witherspoon.

I dont smoke weed, whut u
Talkin about, i did NOT inhale
That weed smoke, i did NOT
Smoke that joint.

If I could be anywhere at the moment?
I'd be some place that's not rainy.
I wish I were in the next room
So I could lie on my couch.

I can't live without
My toothbrush
Or my pit bull
Or my hair straightener
Or my chess set.

I like any sort of food, actually,
But mostly Chinese and cheesesteaks.

In my bedroom, you'll find clothes and a bed,
Some pictures of Brad, and maybe about
84735689317456813 7456 pairs of underwear.

Why should you get to know me?
I dunno, do what you want...
But I tell you what
I am not looking for, though,
Is any man
With a teenie dick.

Why You Should Get To Know Me

I could easily spend the rest of my life
In Disneyland, given the chance. I also crave
Roller coasters—the wilder the better,
And I can't seem to get enough of
Six Flags Magic Mountain.
As a hobby, I write and perform
New Age type music (on the computer),
And I also enjoy writing comedic screenplays.
I'm also HIV/STD.

Go Boo Hoo Hoo

"You're a rich little white girl.
People don't give a damn
About you. They only care about
The poor people, the minorities,
Those less fortunate. Go boo hoo hoo
To Daddy and buy some diamonds.
I'm sure you'll wake up tomorrow
And feel like the million bucks
That's stuck up your ass."

Surprise!

Fickle, unsettled, capricious,
Inconstant as well as vigilant,
Pregnant, eager and watchful,
She picked up the phone and dialed his number.

Unfortunate, threatening, sinister,
Unyielding, hardened, incurable,
Beyond recall, past hope,
Balding, vain and embroiled,
He was also disarrayed and disoriented.
In short, he was irreversible.

Would You Mind?

It's OK that my wife
Likes to suck my titties.
I wish in turn that her hands
Were several sizes larger.
It'd be good to latch on to
Such substantial thumbs.

Years ago, in the parked car,
After much drinking in Winter,
The sad girl said: "Thank you!
It's been so long. I'm going to cry."

The Trojan stayed secreted inside
The imitation leather wallet
For several years, forever,
Until it finally fell apart.

We ate blue fish, she and I,
When the evening was pasted against the sky,
Like two mental patients, naked on the gray carpet.

Lit by a candle, uneaten, the skinny girl
Watched the boy undress, then said,
"I'll lie down next to you, if you don't mind."

If we're still unclaimed a decade from now,
With no one to fondle or pester us,
Would you mind having a baby with me?

Family Planning

We don't have health insurance, baby.
That's why we can't have a baby.
And beside, a baby will certainly ruin
Our cheap new carpet, that's for sure.

On top of that, there are already
6,456,485,175 crapping and polluting,
Rickshaw or SUV steering,
AK-47 or M-16 totting,
Fear Factor and American Idol watching,
Solitary or corporate terrorists jihading
Across this wrecked planet in the name of democracy.

Why would you want to have a baby?

Bad Paintings

I don't care what they say.
There wasn't a bad side to her:
She was always clean;
She always helped us;
And she rode her bike everywhere.
She must have just snapped.

As long as you treated her right, she was good,
But people were always after her thing
And they treated her real bad
So she was always mad at them.

She did say she was going to shoot everybody,
But you'd just go, "Yeah, right." I mean,
Everybody says that sometimes, right?

The truth is
He befriended her many years ago
But their relationship quickly went south
After some argument over a mirror
He was going to give her in exchange
For one of her bad paintings.

The Evil Of Bad Paintings

The problem with bad paintings is that
They are made by bad people.
Simone Weil said that concentration is prayer,
An orientation towards God, and
To paint well takes a hell lot of concentration.
Bad painters, then, are basically people
Who cannot concentrate properly.
Their minds wander as they hold that loaded brush.
Bad painters are not just bad, they're evil.

Made In USA

Aziz had a shaved head, chiseled, with fierce eyebrows.
Born in Iran, he was raised in Germany and England.
When I first met him, I thought he was an ass-kicking painter,
Inspired by Beckman and Kirchner and all those high-strung dudes.
I also considered myself a badass painter then.
Like children, we thought we were destined to rule.
We painted all night, thinking we'll be famous by morning.

What a sweet, angry calling it is—
Wanting to smear your way through life!
Painting as a metaphysical passport to universal acceptance.
Painting as a lift from the mundane and the 9 to 5.
Painting as power and trance and annihilation.

But in our cases, nothing really happened, of course,
As all we had was crazy energy and a love for beer
And a fondness for coke. Only Aziz was certifiably crazy.
Now and then he would lose it for real and end up on the ninth floor
Of Pennsylvania Hospital—the oldest in the country,
Founded by Ben Franklin in 1751.

Everyone always assumed it was drugs that did Aziz in,
But I alone knew it was something else entirely.
Each time he went mad, Aziz would go on about
How he wasn't really Iranian.
How his nose was fake, how even his skin was fake,
How he was a blonde German child kidnapped by Iranian parents.

When Aziz was around blacks, he would say, "I'm black, just like you."
But when he was around whites, he'd say, "I'm white just like you."

On one of his crazy jags, Aziz had this tattooed on his forehead: Made in USA.

Vincent Van Gogh

Impaled with a pitchfork Vincent Van Gogh.
Handcuffed, trussed, and stuffed Vincent Van Gogh.
Decorated with an oversized medal Vincent Van Gogh.
Within the coffin a chintzy suit Vincent Van Gogh.
Domesticated like a rabid hamster Vincent Van Gogh.
Touched up with expensive cosmetics Vincent Van Gogh.
A less-than-life-size statue walks off its base every night in the Jardin D'Arles.

In Print

Any stupid word, once printed,
Will gain immediate authority.
Although I am neither a famous athlete
Nor a movie star nor a politician,
Each day I scan a hundred newspapers
In a dozen languages, hoping
To find my name in print.

Why do I do this?

Maybe there's a mass murderer or a terrorist
With the same name as mine. Or maybe
I've done something spectacular without knowing it.
Or maybe I've died recently without knowing it.
And besides, don't we all deserve to be in print?

Scratched Up

Writing your name means you exist and
You show your strength by how you write it
And you become immortal by writing on the wall.

The Korean shopkeeper and the cholo say:
The soul is always in the line.
Forget the contents, look at the line.
Corporate signs are graffiti in neon.

I myself have taken a class in Oriental calligraphy
At the Pasadena Pacific Asia Museum
Under Yun Chung Chiang,
Himself a student of Pu Ju,
Brother of the last emperor of China.

Lapsarian Rag

We all know that sculptors
Enrich and litter this universe
With their masterpieces.
But what about writers?

The filthy condos they build in our minds
Are also picturesque. And yet
Some of us would rather be an animal.

In nature films, the natives
Are always shunted
From the viewfinder.

The Interstate

The Interstate is a generous and continuous
System of multi-laned highways. It is never
Intersected, not even once, by a lesser road.
One needs not pause on one's life's journey
As long as one's travelling on the Interstate.
It is eternity made real and proven, a diagram
Of heaven (or hell) for the wordless masses.

Exits

These roads were only built
To prevent neighbors from visiting neighbors.

In a vast, empty parking lot,
Orange lights shine on purple asphalt.

The intimacy of my car's interior
Has kept me hopeful for decades now.

We've entered a new level of parking consciousness,
A multitude of multi-level options designed
For the ease of those eager to feast
On noise and monotony and sports.

Idiots are naturally the best drivers—
No inner life, you see,
To distract them from the rules of the road.
(Only geniuses die in car crashes.)

All night long silent trucks deliver goods
From one blank city to another.

Bearings

To sit on one's heels,
With the knees bent
And the weight resting
On the balls of the feet.

To crouch or cower
Close to the ground,
As an animal.

To occupy illegally
An empty, abandoned,
Or condemned building.

Orientals do it.
Occidentals don't.

Baseball catchers and sumo wrestlers also do it.
And a young blonde hiding between two cars
After too many brews on tap,
Her white orbs like twin moons
Inches from the steaming asphalt,
Piddling.

After death I will finally be able to squat
Over my own brown face.

Going Down?

Nothing's safer than what's inside
The pants of what's undesirable.

We'll live forever, Dear, but only
As spectators, as cremated ashes
With eyes, perhaps, inside a jar,

Placed in front of a computer screen.
Ads will pop up. Box scores and death tolls
Will scroll down.

Immortality Is Located In The Sky

I've been on hundreds of airplanes, travelling
To dozens of countries, among young and old
Of every nationality, yet I've never seen
Anyone actually die on an airplane.

Eternity is being strapped to your own spot,
Having to choose between meat and fowl,
Suspended over the Arabian Peninsula,
Aiming for Singapore.

He ruptured his ear drums on take off
Then wheezed his last breath somewhere
Over the blackened Indian Ocean.
(Heaven was bright and he saw his best friend Bob.)
Then he opened his deadened eyes and noticed
That the fastened seat belt sign was still on.

So blunt nosed and so naked
And flying so straight towards
A wished-for destination.

Arrivals and Departures

Transients heaped together, dozing.
A barefoot Aussie wanders off.
Under skylights, a piano sonata.

Mechanical bows in front of a bright store
Selling humanoids, tabloids and beef jerky.

After a week-long junket,
A man fails to recognize his old wife.
An old dog greets the wrong owner.

Years after the filmed explosions,
This airport's still under siege
By sunbaked peasants willing to murder
Their near resemblances for a peep
Of a fat man pushing a cart.

This earth's too narrow, too small, too thin.
The sky's too low for my 5 foot 5 frame.

Soon I'll be 10,000 feet
Or maybe 10,000 miles
Above the Eiffel Tower,
Or the St Louis Arch,
Or the Grand Canyon,
Looking down on you sleeping,
As usual, on your left side,
Hugging nothing.

Dyptich

From an airplane's perspective,
There's no such thing
As a skyscraper.

Kill them all.
Let God sort them out
Later.

Vertigo
Vertigo

He has a muscular torso
With a thousand erections
Lighting up the night sky
But none sticks up more
Than the twin cocks.

(And yet)
Who would think of going all the way
Downtown to castrate
With two knives ablaze?

A muscular story ends.
He now speaks differently
And cannot look into the void
Without flailing.

110

You will live to be 110
On top of a 110-story building
Collapsing finally onto barren land—
Kowtowing like a crippled camel—
Where the temperature will always remain
110 degrees Fahrenheit.

Another Country

Trying to destroy that mural,
The wall collapsed on me,
Crushed my head, broke my neck.
Now I can't even feel myself swallowing.
I've lost my eyesight and my right leg,
Had a hole blown through my left leg,
But I'm glad I tore that wall down.
It was the best experience of my life:
Twenty-one-years old, I've seen two countries.
I was insipid, aimless and poor in bed,
And looking for reasons to take life seriously,
Then I got to play with mines, jump out of airplanes.
I got to interact with another country.

Continuous Bullets Over Flattened Earth

Like horizontal couriers of a vertical fate,
Like troop rotations at a service station,
Like English lessons in Guantánamo,
Like draping towels onto a bronze head,
Like spraying love onto the sand.
I went as one and came back as two.
I went as one and came back as zero.

Etc.?

The revolution revolves,
Is always revolving,
Is hardly a revolution,
Where lumpen are happy
To drape ribbons of flesh
On pyramids of skulls.
Are you low or contemptible?
Unproductive or shiftless?
Alienated or degenerate?

Schema

Apes are encouraged
To wear blue jeans,
Learn English grammar.

Enraged, they blow up
The Capitol Building.

Street to street combat,
Countless civilian corpses,
Civilization burns.

Ape fighters trapped inside
The Jefferson Memorial
Are blown to smithereens
By our own ape soldiers.

I've seen these apes so many times
Wearing T-shirts that don't make sense
Crowding the check out counter at the Wal-Mart.

The President finally appears on TV
To announce that freedom and democracy
Have scorched the forces of evil.

Biters and Gnawers

"I invented what you're packaging.
You should give it at least half the effort
That I did when I made the products."

(I've tried but I'm not the World's Greatest Ass-Kisser.)

Yeah, well, you should have my boot up your ass too.

I have planned on quitting for twelve years now.
I want to quit tomorrow.
But I am so afraid of my boss and his sternness and crap.

The Manager is actually a good-guy type
But he is so strung out on drugs, mostly coke,
That dealing with him is like dealing with Sibyl.

(A bitch oracle in Roman time.)

He called me at the hospital, the motherfucker,
Right after I had my operation, and he asked me
If I could come to work the very next day.

You people are just mean and stupid and you know it.

I spend all my days breathing helium these days
Even though I may be pregnant again.

First of all let me say that
Everyone who knows me says that
I am very friendly and cheery.
I do not say this to blow my own horn
But above all to defend myself.
I actually love helping people and stuff
But it's pretty well all ruined now.

Crime Correctives

Will I be struck by a neon light? A dictionary? A bible?

The intangibles of crime,
Like a bright feather dangling over a small head,
Cast a lurid pall over each citizen's life.

To help the police identify the assailant's voice
During a rape or a homicide, recording devices
Will now be implanted inside the inner ears
Of each citizen.

A camera rigged up behind the citizen's left eyeball
(To photograph the assailant's face) has been rejected
As too expensive and impractical,
As it can easily be dislodged (by said assailant)
With a spoon or a finger.

Night Escape

Inside a locked john in the sky,
Folded into a fugitive fetus,
Among eleven pairs of legs,
Under twelve blankets,
The so-called peace of the grave,
In this pink, perfumed air,
Yearning to shoehorn thirteen inches
Into a bloody, shrunken mitten
Left on a darkened lawn,
Fearful of being dragged
Into the legal light of daybreak.
Can the night itself protect us?

FAQs

Save a puppy?
Or save the planet?

Why pink stinks?

Why can't I get laid on a regular basis?

Why do I prefer
a sweaty, turd-encrusted
garbage hole to a hairy,
beef-swallowing, tuna-
smelling sewer hole?

Why Must I Wash My Hands Every Day?

There is a man, unmarried, bald, with a decent job,
Who must wash his hands each time he touches someone.

In fact, he must wash his hands
Each time he touches a houseplant or a flower,
Or the underside of a dinning room table,
Or the top of his own unmade bed.

He cannot touch any part of his own body
Without washing his hands immediately,
With the most abrasive soap, with a vengeance.

His right hand can never touch his left hand.

At night, this man sleeps with his hands suspended in the air,
Humming a solitary song of ecstasy.

It Was True

She yanked his pants down
To see if it was true, and my God,
It was true: he was wearing his mom's
Old ladies' panties, the pink color fading
A little after so many years but still vibrant,
A lose thread here and there dangling, but
Otherwise the effect was not unbecoming.

A Super Clean Country

You (almost) never see it in public so
You have to conjure it up all day long,
Drag it into every conversation,
To flesh out the corporate picture.

It's an inevitable verbal tic—wouldn't you say?—
For a super-clean country.

Holy shit, that shit's wack.
She thinks she's hot shit but she ain't dogshit.
There's nothing but shit on the internet.
Why are you so hung up on shit like that?
I got some good shit at home, some far-out shit.
You're so full of shit, you dumbshit motherfucker.

Gaining Ashland

Gaining Ashland in the dark, I spotted
A white-bearded dude with a cardboard sign
Next to a glowing sheep.

To continue the resistance,
Old hemp revolutionaries
Must split high-rent San Francisco
To toke up in Ashland,

A Victorian hamlet nestled
Among white-dusted hills,
Once famous for its spring water,
"The purest and healthiest in America,"
Now known for a To Be or We Be Gone Festival
That lasts 9 months a year.

On Main Street, Matisse's nudes
Spin and tumble when not folding clothes.
Catty corner, there's a dilemma,
CD or not CD?

The Moving Stink Spot of Tyson Corner

Old houses, hospitals, and hotels—
As places with deep social histories—
Are very often haunted, yes, but can a
Shopping center also be haunted?

At Tyson Corner, a vast shopping emporium
In suburban Washington, there is a phenomenon
Known as a moving stink spot.

A browser at Foot Locker, for example,
Would suddenly be overwhelmed by a stench
Of open sewage or rotting flesh,
Causing him to retch or even vomit.
This torment would only last for a few seconds, however,
Because the stink spot had already moved on to its next victim.

The shopper can also quickly relieve himself
By simply stepping aside.

The Air In Florida

It is often remarked that people in Florida
Are unusually generous. I can explain:
First,
The air in Florida is always misty with salt.
All metal objects: bicycles, knives, toaster ovens
Are rusted into oblivion within weeks, if not days.
That's why they can afford to give everything away.
When a Floridian hands you the key to his new car,
It's more of a practical joke than an act of generosity.
Secondly, the soil in Florida is piss poor: nothing grows there.
Floridians subsist mostly on scrapple and biscuits.
In countless huts, huge families sleep on plywood platforms
Without electric fans or mosquito netting to ease them through
Another bug-infested, tropical night.
Since Floridians have nothing, they crave everything.
Their elaborate gift-giving is merely folk theater.
A Floridan would hand you a dish towel and say,
This is the wedding dress of the Empress of China.

Right Field Bleachers At Yankee Stadium

The stadium is a womb, one is wrapped in
among one's kind. Faces across the field
are merely flesh.

Sign: WANTED! HOT DOMINICANS TO SPICE UP YANKEES

Another: THERE'S NOTHING LIKE A HISPANIC YANKEE
WILLIAM[S] POSADA MARTINEZ SOJO

Pale geeky guy, with reddish hair
in a pony tail, wearing a tie-dyed T-shirt,
prancing.

Chants from twelve rows behind him:
"Gerry's dead! Gerry's dead!"

The geek licked his middle finger,
then pointed it, nail-ward, at his harassers.

"Gerry's dead! Gerry's dead!"

"Fuck you, bitch! Suck mine!"
Geek started to unbutton his stone-washed jeans.

A brain-dead 50-ish man was escorted from his seat
by two smiling cops. "Buy him another beer!"

A betting pool was started by a pot-bellied guy:
"Only a dollar" on whom will homer first.
"Ladies can play too!"
(If no one guesses right, the house keeps the pot.)

Although smelling like a scam, had many takers.
Most picked the most obvious: Martinez, Strawberry...
Tino went deep in the third.
After paying up, the beer-gut bellowed,
"Now, we do it again!"

Chant: "Ass—hole! Ass—hole!"
at a guy wearing a Mets cap. "Go back to Queens!"
Wads of hot dog wrappers were thrown at the Queenie.

The Dead Head Geek now stood up and started to dance
a serpent dance, undulating.
"Gerry's dead! Gerry's dead!"
His middle finger popped up.
"Sit the fuck down, motherfucker!"
An old black man yelled, stern-faced.

A girl in a red, low cut blouse, all cleavage,
snaked herself up the crowded aisle
to a grand ovation.

She smiled, squinting, waving at the throng,
before her burly boyfriend decided to
kiss his sweet mama for a short eternity
to reclaim his bowling trophy from the hunting pack.
Boooo! "I love you too," someone yelled.

Chant: "Box seats suck! Box seats suck!"

During a pitching change the Tigers' outfield
were huddled in center field, but glaring
at the right field bleachers,
with its chorus of "Fuck you! Fuck you!"
Michigan handshakes all around.

The sun was covered by a cloud for a few seconds: Boooo!
Then uncovered: Cheers!

A guy with a Tigers cap was serenaded
with "Ass—hole! Ass—hole!"
He stood up, smiled, waved, fluttering his pennant.

Chant by five little boys, all in pinstripes:
"People want to knoooow
Whoooo we are?
We are the Yaaankee!
The Yaaankee!
The mighty Yaaankeee!"

On the back of a jacket: "GIVE EM HELL, BILLY!"
[Billy Martin had been dead for ten years.]

Some guy was racing around
with a Tigers cap, apparently snatched
from the head of the Detroit fan.

The cap was tossed around—
"Burn it! Burn it!" the bombshell behind me shrieked—
before being torn into shreds,
before being returned, amid much laughter,
to the infidel.

Baseball Epiphanies

I was so busy screaming,
I didn't even see all those
Amazing home runs.

That dumbshit third base coach
With a fuckin windmill for a left arm
Has just cost us another fuckin ballgame.

A slap hitting wuss with a yen for sliding headfirst into oblivion.

A life-long slump
On the mound and at the plate
Without, strangely enough,
Being demoted even once
To the minors.

That dude could not bunt, bat, run, field or throw
But he had all the intangibles down.

This man got up
This morning, went to work,
Kissed
His wife
Goodbye,
And from what I heard, he was caught
In a horrible suicide squeeze.
I'm just devastated.

I know everyone's (updated) batting average,
The stockbroker's, the butcher's, the mailman's,
But my own.

Standing on the on-deck circle,
Getting ready to vindicate myself,
I suddenly realized that
The lights had long been turned off
And the stadium was empty.

Sudden Death Overtime

I stiff-armed my way through
An army of lunging assholes,
Sidestepping bouncing betties,
Just so I could kiss once more
That line of scrimmage.

Badly booted,
The wobbly pigskin, skimming
The frozen ground, barely
Cleared the tilting uprights
Of my father's grave.

This Sporting Life

As the temperature dips, the green jackets come out.
Walking down a deserted South Street
At 10:30 AM on Sunday, October 3rd,
I saw a green jacket, 40-ish, talking to himself.
Nothing wrong with that—I do it all the time.
I slowed my pace to catch his every word:

"They're going to fuck up again—they always do.
They may beat the Bears today but that won't even
Get my damn dick hard!"

Couldn't agree with him more.

Though we won later that day, 19-10,
Outrushing them 154-32,
Outpassing them 222-118,
My hellbound sleuth never turned to stone at the final whistle.

Immersions

I will dip (bread, cake, etc.)
Into coffee or other liquid.
Or rather, I will score an accented field goal
By leaping and thrusting a big brown ball
Down the throat of a well-hung, braided basket.
Nothing's more beautiful in this blighted world
Than a well-hung, braided basket—
A polyester chute.

With your hands in my face,
I will gently leap.

Stats

We do points per game and shooting percentage, of course,
And steals and assists and yards per carry
And fumbles and sacks and penalty minutes.
We tally all of our punches because it's very important
That we quantify each moment of our murderous lives.
A man must be accountable for all of his thrills and fuckups.
We also do girls and countries but we don't do collateral damages.

Fifteen Rounds With A Nobody

I can only show my happy self
To A, and my angry self to B;
Thus, when I'm with both A and B,
I do not know how to behave.

Jolted by an unpleasant memory,
I punch myself—hard!—in the face.

In my defense I can only say:
"The point is universality and solidarity.
Unity, transparency, efficiency,
Collectivity and objectivity.
These are the key words."

Devastation

Yes, I have moments. Sometimes
I'd think it's only a vehicle,
A means to an end, but then I'd realize
How much I love it, in spite of the atrocities.
As soon as I'm walking down the street,
And I see, for example, whatever,
Everything just burns me up.

I've paid my dues all these years but no one
Pays attention. No one knows the fuck who I am.
It's a weird life, man, it's very lonely.
But everyone needs his privacy, you know.
When people look at me, all they see is
A gatecrasher and a fuckin weirdo.

A person may not have the money
Or the power or the love
Or the peace of mind, but that doesn't mean
He's a victim. No one's a victim.
After an unfortunate coincidence,
You've just got to say, Fuck it!
And move on.

You know how it is: everybody's below average,
But everybody wants to be a star.
Who said you're entitled to an income?

There's no guarantee, you know, there's no God.
Living in a big house and eating all the time is way overrated.
I remember when they arrested me and gave me a cavity check
And took everything I had away, I felt relieved.
There was nothing for me to do but to gain weight.

It's so ironic but when I grew up
We didn't have shit for dinner.
I've slept in holes you wouldn't throw up in.
Since then I've never had less than a million in the bank.
When I first got here, I wanted to eat everything up:
I wanted to drink all the wine and chase all the women.

I guess it's halfway an insecurity thing.
I guess at a certain age you start to feel like
You're ready to hang out with your offspring,
And when your offspring start saying things like,
"I love you, Daddy," you can't help but think, "Fuck!
Does that mean I'm an old man?"

It took me forever to figure it out,
You know, like, Shit!
If you gonna have kids,
Then you're going to die,
But you must also believe in the future.

Talking about the future, you see that snowman standing outside?
I built it with my offspring just yesterday morning,
But it's practically gone already.
You see that carrot lying there on the grass?

Give Me Some

Cruising South Philly, I'm always on the lookout
For virgins. I ain't getting nothing in this life,
So goes the reasoning, I might as well
Get some in the next life.

There she is, at 10th and Dickinson,
Rising above a bed of red carnations,
Her stony foot crushing a stone serpent.

At 12th and Reed, she appears six times
In one window, alone or with her baby,
Or cradling a dead man.

At Giordano, she hovers behind the counter,
Spreading her mantle.

At 9th and Wilder, she's not so much
Virgin as goddess—aren't they all?—
Encased in crazed plexiglas
With her right hand pointing skyward.

The same goddess, supersized,
Rules the corner of 13th and Washington,
Planted on a lotus and guarded by two lions.

Belle donne tutte, all these fine ladies,
Italiane o cinesi, and all proving that the cult
Of the goddess is very much alive in South Philly.

APIC

If Basie and Ellington could call themselves Count and Duke,
Then Lee Goldston had every right to declare himself President
Of the Associated Philadelphia International Company.
He even had cards embossed to impress his clients.
But all APIC was was Lee with a squeegee and a bucket,
Making the rounds of Center City stores to do their windows.
Whenever I was seriously hurting, I'd join Lee's firm.
Though he had lined up all the gigs, Lee never hesitated
To give me half of the day's take—usually around 40 bucks.
It wasn't too bad a job in warm weather but in midwinter,
Water sometimes froze on glass before you could even scrape it.
A stooping black man in plastic shades and mangy beret,
Lee thrived on liquid yeast—like all of us—and when he died,
No one found out about it until a week later, not until
The landlord came to his apartment to collect the late rent.

Lucre

Of all the grunts and beer bellies I knew in Philly,
I have always wanted to describe Joe LeBlanc.
(But I don't want to distort or slander him in any way.)
As my house painting boss, he kept me alive
During my most desperate years. When there was no work,
He would lend me money or give me money outright.
Born in Quebec, Joe had gone South to join the US Army.
During the Vietnam War, he was a gunner on an Army chopper,
Spraying generous lead over coned heads and pock-marked jungles,
Before he became disgruntled and was dishonorably discharged.
In Saigon, Joe had a girlfriend who was half-French.
"Half yellow and half white is the best combo," Joe said.
"Half yellow and half black is no doubt the worst."
Joe would hire anyone: an old man, a fat woman,
Even a punk or a drug addict, but never a black person.
Joe often slurred black children but he also gave
New bikes and eyeglasses to black kids living on his street.
Joe bought novels at K-Mart and Seven Eleven.
Occasionally he'd toss baseball cards behind dry walls
As gifts for future boys and dry-wallers…
Married once, Joe was living with a brown mutt by then.
In the evening you'd find him alone at his kitchen table,
Drunk on whiskey and crossing out with a Magic Marker
The "in God we trust" from all the bills in his possession.
Joe's dream was to retire to a dome home in Kentucky,
Where he could drink and fire his weapon repeatedly
Into infinity.

Eating Fried Chicken

I hate to admit this, brother, but there are times
When I'm eating fried chicken
When I think about nothing else but eating fried chicken,
When I utterly forget about my family, honor and country,
The various blood debts you owe me,
My past humiliations and my future crimes—
Everything, in short, but the crispy skin on my fried chicken.

But I'm not altogether evil, there are also times
When I will refuse to lick or swallow anything
That's not generally available to mankind.

(Which is, when you think about it, absolutely nothing at all.)

And no doubt that's why apples can cause riots,
And meat brings humiliation,
And each gasp of air
Will fill one's lungs with gun powder and smoke.

Going to Goa

Living in such an impoverished, degraded world,
He rationalized his riches by becoming an artist.
Buying into this, he never apologized.
The idea was to spend whatever that was necessary.
Going to Goa was warranted because it was stimulating
And because it fleshed out his knowledge about Goa.
Eating a souffle in front of a child beggar
Was necessary for a future souffle painting.
Sucking blood with a straw, the father's corruption
Was necessary to elevate the artist son.
An artist cannot waste money
Because money cannot be wasted on an artist.
He should be showered with money,
As much money as possible,
Even blood money.

Glockenspiel

Sorry, bath water! Sorry, sofa!
Sorry, dark woman wearing a hat!
Sorry, chipped monument to the year 2,000!
Sorry, stiff salute! And, again, so sorry!
Words misheard, then misforgotten, then misremembered!
Mattress without appendix! Unnamed flowers!
Classified insects, my sincerest apologies.
(Brightest things, why are we so beautiful?)
All is possible, dear, but later,
After the fact, and for that,
My sincerest apologies.

Yes You Heard Me

A heart lying on its side,
Under a spent strobe light,
Dreaming of a locked zoo,
Dreaming of a blocked bladder,
Dreaming of a vast nocturama
Where one can meander naked
For the rest of one's span
Without bumping into one's shadows,
Dreaming of scoring a ticket
To the top of the skull tower
From a scalper skull.

Phallic Stanzas

Bush
Exploding
Bush

Words
Are never appropriate
Words

In youth
I loved myself so much
In youth

A nose
Like a semi colon
A nose

Alive
Did I hear you were still
Alive?

Nuts
Don't always have to be
Symmetrical

What's Wrong With American Literature?

Drunk #1: Readers are no longer interested
In experimental hogwash. They want real stories
About real people, concerning real things
That really matter.

Drunk #2: Writers should learn how to dish up
Small tales about myopic people
With a dim view of happiness
(And how come none of us has it).

Drunk #3: A writer must be well-versed
In making us forget where and who we are,
At least for the duration of the book.

Drunk #4: No philosophy nor politics,
No ideas whatsoever, only moods.

Drunk #5: A reader from Mackville, Vermont
Reading a novel about Mackville, Vermont,
By a novelist from Mackville, Vermont.

Drunk #6: Inspirational tales delivered with a chuckle!

Drunk #7: I, on the other hand, write poems
About my father's hands, my mother's breasts.

Drunk #8: What will it matter in the end—
So many words on a flickering screen,
In front of a flickering mind?

Pentameters

Umm so 2 days ago we had my mom's
Services and it was really sad. I
Saw a bunch of people I hadn't seen
In a long time. My old friend Brittney looked
Pretty hot actually. (I'm just messing
With u Kristen!) So I saw my best friend
Who I haven't talked to in like a year.
His name is Brenden. We have been best friends
Since we were three. We decided to start doing
More stuff together cus we never see
Each other anymore. He gave a little
Speech thing that made me feel a lot better
And it made me respect him a lot more.
I never realized how emotional
He was. I never saw him break down in
Tears like that and I never really wanted
To see him do that but it shows how much
He cares. Umm I could easily tell that
Kristen liked him. She was staring at his
Crotch the whole time. Umm yeah and I just got
To catch up with everybody and
Kristen got to meet some of my friends. O
We had this big line of pics of my mom
When she was younger and stuff and Brenden
Came up to me and actually told me
"Damn your mom was hot" and I told him back
"Yeah I know." It felt kind of creepy to
Say that especially cus she's dead and
She was probably listening to us
And she is my mom but she was pretty
Attractive. So I asked him if she still

Looked like that and was still alive would he
Hit on her and he said yes. Brenden is
Like one of the most honest guys I know
(Just cus he doesn't really care what people
Think of him) but he never takes care of
Himself. He only takes like five showers
A month and the weirdest thing about that
Is they're all on the same day. O and he
Has a girlfriend but he says that they're going
Through "rough times" cus he bit her on the ass.
Y would you bite a girl on the ass? Does
It taste good? Do girls find that erotic
Or pleasurable? Was she constipated
And Brenden was just trying to motivate
Her to get the rest out? O Kristen my
Grandpa says ur a fine young woman and
He says ur quite a catch. I think he ODs
On viagra or horny goat weed cus
He's like the horniest guy I know and
He's like 70 or 80. O he
Also said "I'd like to have that bitch buff
My fucking pickle." Sorry that was just
A joke. Y were u surprised that I knew
The reasons y u wore a skirt? I'm not
That stupid and anyone could realize
The advantages of it. It only
Makes u look less slutty to the parents
So they will be less suspecting but it
Allows easier access. Anyone
With a brain could figure that out. OK I
Better stop typing cus I'm just rambling

On. I'll go now. I haven't been able
To sleep lately and it's really pissing
Me off. P.S. Before u guys go I
Have a joke Q: Why do aliens always
Probe you in the ass? A: Because the
First person ever abducted was a British
Man and they asked him where he would like it
The most and he replied "Up Me Arse. Stick
It Up Me Arse." And another joke Q:
What's the difference between a British
Man and a British woman? A: A
British woman has a higher sperm count.
Hahahahaha sorry those r just
Too funny. No offense to any British
Women, just the men.

Tourism

I see you here every night drinking by yourself.
Why did you come to this country?
What do you want? Ganja?
To sleep with a little boy or a little girl?
To pose in front of a burnt out tank in the middle of an open field?
The tail of a bomber sticking out of a pond?

But the tanks and planes are all gone, unfortunately.
Our peasants dismantled them and sold them for scraps.
They also dismantle unexploded bombs and sell them for scraps.
Although we're not good at building things, we know how to take things apart.
We can dismantle New York City in half an hour and sell it for scraps.

The explosive from a single bomb can be sold for 450 bucks,
An equivalent of a year's salary.
But for that, you have to dig down 40 feet.
Colorful cluster bombs, however, are right on the surface
And can be picked up by children.

That's one thing we're perversely proud of:
Our ability to dig into the ground.
Other nations boast of building up.
We boast of building down.

From inside the oval window, from above,
What were your first impressions flying in?
That our streets are like worms or bodies fucking?
Maybe the plane will never land, you started to hope.
Maybe it could circle forever over this baffling country.
Our interaction would be limited to you dropping flyers, books, and flowers
From above the clouds.

But before you knew it, you were in it, you were inside our country.

Were you impressed by our skyscrapers?
We built a few just to show we're modern.
But no one lives or works in them.
They don't have elevators, plumbing or electricity.
There are rumors they don't exist at all,
Just images projected into the sky by some machine.

Guests at our most famous hotel are told they're not allowed
To place their hands under the blanket.
They must show their hands at all time or the bellhop
Will rap them on the forehead.

See the white guy at that table?
From your country, Florida.
He's lived here for over three years
And is always talking about his wife "Lan,"
But none of us has ever seen her.
We all know the old soldier lives alone.

Is Lan a prostitute from 30 years ago?
A maid who sneaks into his room at night?
A ghost he gropes under the blanket after he's turned off the light?

As you can see, he's only half a man,
Though I'm not sure which half he's missing.

Do you fantasize about the war?
Sorry you weren't in it?
Your life is meaningless because you've never been shot at?
Do you want to spend a night in jail just to see what it's like?
Do you want to buy an M-16 or an AK-47?
A hundred twenty five bucks is all it takes.
Twenty-five cents a bullet.

I hear half of your vets are turning into suicidal psychos.
They wake up in the middle of the night screaming, "Don't drink the water!"
They stand on street corners with cardboard signs saying: "Will Kill for
Food."

Are you falling asleep on me? What's the matter?
You need to throw up? How many whiskies have you had?
I thought you guys could put away gallons of this stuff.

Glad to have you back, my friend.
I thought you've passed out in the bathroom in a puddle of vomit.
How do you like the graffiti over the urinal:
To shoot at something and see it bounces away from you
Is like having your dick reach eternity?

This bar is not too bad, actually. It was designed
For folks like you to feel right at home.
Everything passes by and you're surrounded by your own kind.

Quick, how many kinds are there?

The Death Of English

It stang me to sang of such thang:
This language, like all others, will be deep fried,
Will die, then be reborn as another tongue
Sloshed in too many mouths. What of
"That kiff joint has conked me on a dime"?
"Them cedars, like quills, writing the ground"?
It's all japlish or ebonics, or perhaps Harold Bloom's
Boneless hand fondling a feminist's thigh.

Urban Warfare

It's August in July and I'm lying on my belly,
Reading a John Ashbery poem, facing outward
Into the terrace of a third floor walk-up
I share with the wife, a student of English-

As-a-secondhand-language at the Y.M.C.A.,
Where you can get an excellent meal, do whatever you feel,
And where young men groove all days of the week.
As Sir Elton John wails from a neighbor's radio,

And the Olympics comes on live on TV,
My eyes tail a meandering ant down the page
From "inner stress, sheltered from the cold"
To "swallowed everything with his knives."

This quality time with my favorite wry uncle
Cannot even be ruined by four large trash bags
Filled with soiled cat litter and left on the terrace
For more than a month now, by our burly neighbor, Pat.

After John Skelton

JUST JUNK IT! JUNK IT! JUNK IT NOW!
You are a dumb piece of ass.
You teased me with your tailfeather.
You have VERY nice buns.
I hate your combustion, you dumb fuck!
You're the last surviving member of the breed.
You amazed and dazzled me.
Kudos and butterfly kisses.
Unworthy.
I hate that you love Diaperman more than me.
I realize he's the captain of your shrimp boat
and I'm a mere Greek bottler, but please,
I want to do the elephant walk with you again.
Ta Ta.
Wow! You sucked me into your world.
You teased me with your tailfeather.
I kissed your toes.
You ain't never gonna get a man. You.

Vocab Lab

This word means yes,
however, maybe, or no,
depending on the situation.

This word means desire,
love, friendship, rape, or a sudden urge
to engage someone in a philosophical
conversation.

This word is unlearnable,
its meaning hermetic to all outsiders.
It can neither be pronounced
nor memorized.

This word is protean and can be spelled
an *inifinite* number of ways.
Its meaning, however, is exact.

This word is also protean,
and may be used in place of any other word,
without loss of meaning.

This word can only be hinted at, implied,
and thus appears in no books,
not even in a dictionary.

This word can neither be spoken nor seen.
It can be freely written, however,
but only in complete darkness.

This word means one thing when spoken by a man,
and another thing, altogether different, when said by a woman.

This word means now, soon, or never,
depending on the age of the speaker.

This word means here, there, or nowhere,
depending on the speaker's nationality.

It has often been said that the natives
will only teach foreigners a fake, degraded language,
a mock system of signs
parodying the real language.

It has also been said that the natives
don't know their own language,
and must mimic the phony languages of foreigners,
to make sense out of their lives.

Living Among You People

Over the years, I've picked up
A word or two, maybe even a thousand,
Although my syntax, admittedly,
Could use a bit of emendation.

I may be colorblind and inarticulate,
But I can see everything from *below*,
From my vantage point on the tiled floor,
Where I often pretend to sleep.

Sometimes I'd really be sleeping,
But at the slightest acoustic disturbance,
A drunken invective spat out a mile away,
Sweet nothings whispered in a drunken dream,
Or a lizard sighing,
And I'd be awake again.

I can see the dead as well as the living.
They talk to me and pat me on the head.
They toss me imaginary bones.
Although they like to wander across the earth,
They always return to their old haunts at night,
The way ducks return to their pen.

They do not haunt this planet for very long.
Out of fear, habit, and tenderness,
All would try to fend off oblivion,
Before they consent to disappear.

x

Where my home used to be,
Where my face used to be,

Always firm and frontal,
It has become my first and last name.

It is the only word I know.
Behind this x sign here

Is another x sign (here),
Perched on a swirly stool,

Coy, exasperated,
Waiting for that final x.

About the Author

Linh Dinh is the author of two collections of stories, *Fake House* (Seven Stories Press 2000) and *Blood and Soap* (Seven Stories Press 2004), and two books of poems, *All Around What Empties Out"* (Tinfish 2003) and *Borderless Bodies* (Factory School 2005). His work has been anthologized in *Best American Poetry 2000* (Scribner 2000), *Best American Poetry 2004* (Scribner 2004) and *Great American Prose Poems from Poe to the Present* (Scribner 2003), among other places. He is also the editor of the anthologies *Night, Again: Contemporary Fiction from Vietnam* (Seven Stories Press 1996) and *Three Vietnamese Poets* (Tinfish 2001).